Out of Brokenness

KENEATHA RENAE

Written by Keneatha Renae

Foreword by Kyandra Knight

Cover design by Kevon Knight

Edited by Candace Stewart, Collab Network, LLC

BLACK&BARE PRESS

© Black&Bare Press, 2021.
All rights reserved.

No part of this book may be used or reproduced in any manner whatsoever without written permission from the publisher except in the case of brief quotations embodied in critical articles or reviews.

For information, contact us at
blacknbare@gmail.com

Published by Black&Bare Press
Names: Keneatha Renae, author.
Title: Out Of Brokenness / Keneatha Renae
www.blacknbarepress.com

Out of Brokenness

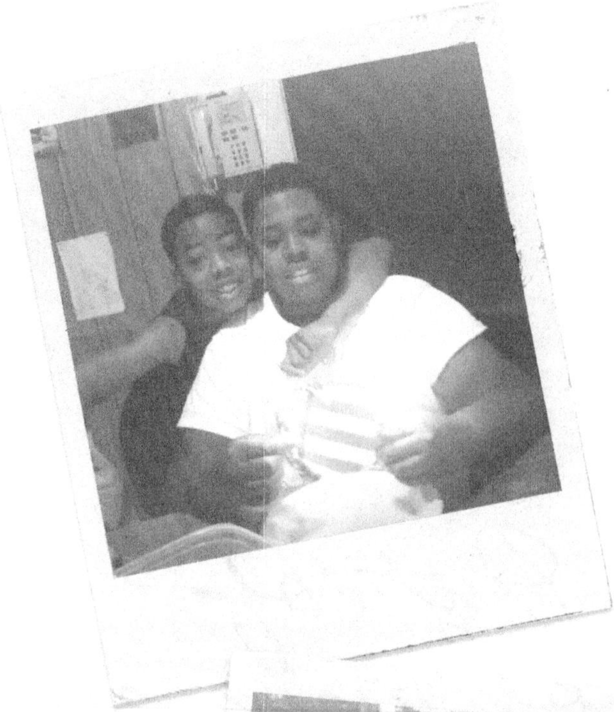

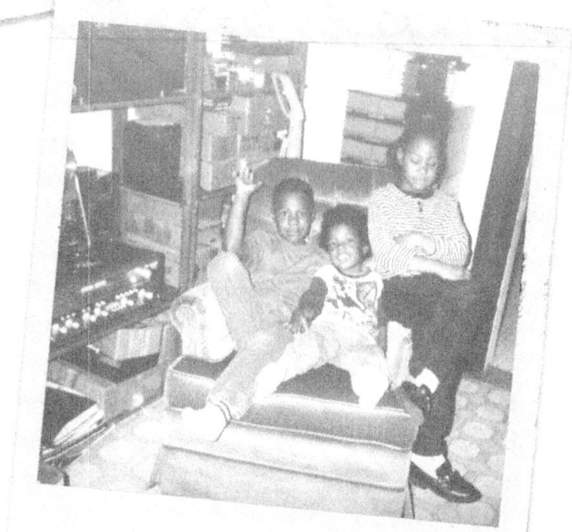

I dedicate this labor of love, and exercise in healing to my children, who have encouraged me to follow my dreams since forever. Their infectious smiles and laughter, joy and tears, their steadfast belief and love in and for me have sustained me through each dark night and every bright new day. I am a better person because of the gift of their existence, and I thank them for believing in me when I had lost the capacity and will to believe in myself. For all of that and more, they are forever my greatest joy and blessing. And everything I am stems from the gift of love that is their very existence.

Contents

Foreword	8
Preface	10
Out of Brokenness	14
Daddy	16
It's my Fault	20
I Miss You	22
Again	24
Carolyn Cousins	28
Yeah, I Hungry	30
Daughter	32
I Was Born in Magic	34
No Reply	38
You're the Dopest	40
Niggas Aint Shit	42
Black Shit	44
The Other Side of Here	46
The World is Burning	50
A Prayer	52
Tiny World	54
Loss	56

Lost In The Beat	58
The Phone Call	60
God Saved Me	62
Heartbroken	64
We Used To Be	66
Summer	68
Mother	70
Strength through Observation	74
The Gaps You Left Behind	76
A View Too Close	82
I Can't With You	86
Perspective	88
Longing	90
Thoughts of You	92
Finding Out	94
Moonlight Dance	98
Unbreaking Brokenness	100
Acknowledgments	106
About the Author	108

Foreword

Held close to my heart is a vague memory of laying on the floor, laughing with my brothers in a modest room, not mine but ours, missing nothing of critical importance. I did not remember the dimensions of the room, only that they were enough to laugh comfortably in. I did not remember the items in the room, only that they were enough to play with. A room that was ours positioned close to another room that was ours, but that was also shared with a family, a friend, perhaps a stranger depending on who needed it. Looking back, I suppose the rooms were small, but I could race toy cars across their floors without the need for more racing ground. I could lay out and kick my feet back and read, or write, and how I loved to write just like my mama, without feeling as though I were cramped. I knew from television and other families' homes and sometimes from the hunger in my belly that there were bigger rooms in the world, but I never felt stifled in stretching out. The world always seemed massive to me, and I felt that I could dream and eventually attain anything I wanted even if I didn't have it then, so I was not pressed. This is a testament to the great imagination that flourishes with the right facilitation. Out of brokenness, my mother catalyzed imagination within me. In the book, she writes, we were poor, and yeah, we were. But we were rich in love, and that makes material riches look pitiful in hindsight.

As a small child, I knew what it meant to share and have enough: to share love, shelter, and food no matter the amount there was to go around. I have always known what it is to be in community, and I later learned the sacrifice involved and that, out of brokenness, sometimes arrives wherewithal to build up ourselves and others. Sometimes out of brokenness comes a commitment towards repair and reconstruction. I believe my mother reconstructed the world around me each and every day. My world was open to endless possibilities out of brokenness. I later learned that some things are not attainable through a dream, determination, or 'hard work' but through the systemic deconstruction of inequity. I also learned a framework to navigate the world with a sense of community and joy despite any adversity to do just that. Out of her brokenness, my mother illustrated joy in darkness and a commitment to community.

Sometimes people close themselves off to the world and others when there is not enough to go around or when they are hurt and wronged. That is a valid position. For my mother, there was always more to go around if someone was in need. Out of Brokenness is yams, cornbread, and Mac and Cheese, too much for the soul to eat up in one serving.

When we were growing up, I was taught there was always more to share. It was only later in my life that I characterized that we were poor and on the wrong side of town in the early days, but we were raised in the security and safety, and riches of my mother's wisdom, brilliance, and love.

Out of brokenness, my mother presented to my siblings and me a world that was fundamentally rooted in community, fundamentally rooted in the idea that if one of us ate, we all ate. Out of brokenness, my mother put food on our table and food in our minds and spirits.

Just as I have always known what it is to give without expectation, to share, and to have enough through her example, I have always known joy: a thing which has a way of finding you deep in darkness and despair; a thing that can exist alongside and stick to pain and grief like a magnet. It is with great joy that I write to you, reader, in my voice which has been so thoroughly shaped by my mother's, about Out of Brokenness, which is in my opinion, a tale of sharing, of growth, of pain, of hurt, and joy.

Sometimes bad things happen to us. Sometimes they break us. Sometimes they build us. Sometimes they leave us numb. Sometimes they do all of those things at once. Out of Brokenness is a truth-telling of things that happen. You may feel broken, numb, agitated, angry, hurt, and joy through its reading. All of that is valid. It is an exhalation of strength. It is a grand and soft and present declaration: "I have come out on the other side, I have felt, and I have contributed love to others in turn." My mother and her decision to share her stories are an illustration of strength and grace. I hope you connect. I hope you cry. I hope you sigh. I hope you get angry. I hope you leave this book imagining limitless worlds and dreaming possibilities out of smallish rooms.

I can never characterize accurately how beautiful my mother is in words. Still, when I read Out of Brokenness, I felt affirmed that the burning ball of light inside me that threatens to escape me, shattering my limbs upon exit with joy when I think of her, was valid. I felt myself wanting to go back in time and protect her from every Bad Thing, the way she so gracefully positioned herself to do for me time and again despite every Bad Thing. I felt inspired and hopeful. May the words in this book light a fire in you to love yourself deeply, know you are worthy and know that it is possible to come out of your brokenness for no one else but you.

It is also with particular joy that I celebrate with you the words in the book, the words themselves because it was my mother who taught me that we build our world through our words. It is she who positioned me to fall in love with writing, who introduced this art to me, and who inspires me to use my words for liberation and movement work today. Take a breath and position yourself to go in deep. Now get reading!

Kyandra Knight

Foreword

Preface

    This project has been in the making all my life. Before I even realized it, it was always there. I've written poems, short stories, commentaries on my life and the world around since forever. A running dialogue of reflection. For myself. Tucked away in drawers, notebooks in keepsake boxes, scraps of paper tucked into books and crevices any and everywhere. I've always wanted to publish a collection of those thoughts, but it never seemed to be the right time or never seemed to be affordable or attainable. Life demanded my focus, so I kept putting it off. And then the pandemic happened. And I realized there was never going to be the right time. The perfect time for things to line up in perfection didn't exist. I realized that all the reasons why I hadn't done this before were excuses. If I wanted this to go from dream to reality, I had to let go of all the reasons why I couldn't do it and grab onto the reasons why I not only could but should. I realized that all the days that you think you have to do it later might never materialize. Now is all that we have, and I wanted to use my Now moments to pursue every dream I've ever had.

—Starting with this one.

There is no rhyme or reason for the following pages.
No smooth transition from love to hate to healing or wholeness.
There is only the expression of human emotion.

Erratic.

    Chaotic.

                  Messy.

           Beautiful.

                        Raw. **Real.**

Honest.

              Laid bare.

                      Vulnerable.

A journey that I hope that you walk away from feeling visible and seen.
Hopeful and drained.

                Alive.

All at the same time.

Out of Brokenness

Keneatha Renae

Out of Brokenness

Out of brokenness
I was shaped;
Formed
Shattered
Pieces of me
Still missing
Buried
Beneath pain
Shame
Lack
Feelings of not enough
And being unworthy

Too short
Too fat
Too skinny
Too loud
Too quiet
Too broken

Labels that others draped around me
And I clutched them close to me
Because they felt familiar
They were what I was used to

Pieces
Buried
Hidden
Missing
But existing as if I was whole
Even though I wasn't
Because it was all I ever knew

Daddy

Daddy

Daddy

I can't remember the first time you touched me.
I remember bits and pieces of moments of tears and pain.
Moments that should have never occurred.
Me sitting on your lap.
You kissing me.
A little girl, maybe 8 or 9 years old.

The thought makes me sick.
Even now.
I feel anxious.
Overwhelmed.
Scared.
I felt then.
Dirty.
Confused.
Ashamed.

I remember waking up to you on top of me.
3 times my height and size.
Tears streaming down my face.
You telling me to go back to sleep.
Your little girl.
That, I enjoyed it more when I was asleep.
I was 10 years old.
10 Years Old!

I remember you taking me on trips out of town.
Stopping at roadside places.
Pulling me into sleeping bags.
At the back of parking lots.
Away from lights.
And people.

Daddy

Touching.
Groping.
Forcing.
Pain.
Unbearable.
Physical.
Spiritual.
Emotional.
Pain.
Unspeakable.

I remember you saying I couldn't tell.

I would destroy our family if I told.
I would be blamed if I told.
You would kill the people I loved if I told.
No one would believe me if I told.
So I didn't.
Tell.
For a long time.
Until the fear of you and what you did.
Over and over again.
Outweighed the fear of your threats.
So I did tell.
In a whisper. Not a shout.
Still afraid. Still unsure.
Still feeling at fault.
And even though I told I didn't tell everything.
It was too hard.
The looks.
The shame.
The whispers.
As if I didn't understand.
As if *I* shared blame.
For your actions.
For your crime.

Daddy

But I told enough.
But you were still the person I knew as "dad."
And I struggled with hate and love.
And when I thought I had finally found a place of enough healing, you asked to speak to me.
From behind bars.
Over the phone.
Miles away.

And I was still afraid.
And felt sick.

But I did.
Speak to you.
For just a moment.
And your words crushed me even more than your actions.
I forgive you, you said.
You told me that You forgave *Me*.
I forgive you
For sending me to jail.
You said.
I couldn't understand.
The pain.
The shock.
I dropped the phone.
Whatever healing had taken place was shattered.
And I was that little girl again.
Hiding.
Trying not to be seen.
So you wouldn't notice.
So you wouldn't single me out for attention I never wanted.
Wasn't old enough to understand.
Wasn't mature enough to process.
Shattered. Broken. Ashamed.

It's My Fault

It's My Fault

It's my fault, not yours
I said it was okay
When I stayed
After the first time
You hit me
You cheated
You stole from me
From us
From our children
It's my fault, not yours
I taught you that it was okay
To lie
That I would accept it
That I would pretend that it was the truth
It's my fault, not yours
That in loving you
I forgot how to love me
It's my fault, not yours
That I've just now awakened
And realized what you always knew
That it was your fault all along

Miss You!

I miss you
The sound of you
The look
The feel
I miss knowing
Confidently
That you were there
I don't even remember when I lost you
Or if I ever truly had you for more than
Brief
Fleeting
Moments
You seem so distant
Yet so close
If I could just reach you
If you could just come back to me
I would never let you go
I'd cherish you
Hold you close
Nurture you
Let you run free
I'd let you scream and shout
And never
Ever
Let you go again

Again

Again

I said I would never be in this place again
Of pain
Of brokenness
Of hurt
but here I am

Lost
Alone
Shattered
I was so careful
I thought
I had boundaries
I thought
I had a wall that was supposed to protect me
I thought
But brick by brick, you removed that wall
I didn't even notice
One lie
That didn't seem like a lie
One mistake
Explained away
One nasty voicemail or text or conversation
Because you were upset
You didn't mean it
You cheated because of *me*
You said
I didn't pay enough attention
I expected too much
You couldn't change overnight
This is who you were for so long
Be patient.
You said
You loved me
    you said

Again

I believed when I shouldn't have
Turned a blind eye when I shouldn't have
Ignored
Sometimes not knowing
Sometimes on purpose
I just wanted peace
Quiet
A break from the constant pain
I thought I was doing it because I wanted peace

I didn't realize
Not really
That peace was not what I was creating
I was creating
Acceptance
Tolerance
Of things, I *never* should have
I was trying desperately
To save you
To get you to be the person I thought I saw you were capable of being
While losing every bit of me
I didn't know
Not really

Again

I thought I would never be here again
I thought I was protecting myself
I thought I was smarter this time
I thought I was more careful

But I wasn't

Carolyn Cousins

There were many of us
In the same bed
Fighting over who slept next to who
Cause no one wanted to sleep next to the one that peed in the bed

We stayed up all night
Fashion shows with gowns and scarves
Talent shows with notebook paper
Everyone took it so seriously
Scoring each other's act
Giving feedback
We played hide and seek
And volleyball in the backyard
We caught tadpoles in the creek
And rode our bikes down Church Hill.

Carolyn Cousins

We were sisters and cousins
And more
We didn't have much
But each other
That felt like more than enough
We cried together
Shared secrets

Laughed and laughed and laughed
At anything and everything
We fought and made up
And fought and made up
And then we went outside and made hamburgers
 out of mud and leaves
And french fries out of twigs
And licked on freeze cups made with Kool-Aid as sweet as molasses
And walked to Ben Franklin
for penny candy that was gone before we returned home.
And we talked
And laughed and laughed and laughed
We didn't have anything
But we had each other

And that felt like more than enough

Yeah, I Hungry

We were poor
I mean no food at night poor
I mean, once the food stamps ran out
Middle of month poor
We made do with what we had
Heads of lettuce
Watered down mayonnaise
Seasoned with salt and pepper
Better than any salad we could have dreamed of
Cause it was something
All we had

Free breakfast and lunch at school
Hiding the telltale orange card
That told everyone else
We were poor
Couldn't even afford food
Free lunch in the summer at the Gil
The community center in Cincinnati
Sometimes
Oftentimes
The only meal we got

Yeah, I Hungry

Boxes with cold bread
Colder lunch meat
Juice
Cookies
Chips
Felt like heaven
We always saved something
Just in case
For later
In case there was nothing else
Often there was nothing else
We made candy on the stove
Sugar and butter
Freezing it
Anxious for it to be ready
We made do with what we had
We had no other choice
Seemed normal
It was all we knew
We watched TV
Distracting us from empty bellies
Watching commercials with food
Was hard
Sitting on the living room floor
Cold tile
Burger King commercials
Asking, "Aren't you hungry?"
My baby sister saying, "Yeah, I hungry."
We laughed.
Nervously.
But we laughed
With empty bellies
Cause she said what we'd all felt
Yeah, we hungry
But we made do with what we had
We didn't have another choice
It was all we knew

Out of Brokenness

Daughter

The first time I saw you
I felt as if I couldn't breathe
I felt like my heart stopped
The world around me shifted
I had no concept of what I was feeling
The immediate hope
And fear

I knew that I would love you
Forever
And ever
I didn't think anyone could ever
Not ever
Have felt this before
This longing
And desire
To be close to you
To feel your breath on my cheek
To feel the touch of your skin
It overwhelmed me

Daughter

You were perfect
Tiny
Amazing
Fierce
Already
There was a passion in your eyes
Determined
Decided
Even then
I knew not only would I die for you
I'd live my life forever
For you

In that moment
When we first met
I knew
For the first time
Really
There was a God
And that He loved me
Because no other explanation could explain
The gift of you

I Was Born in Magic

I was born in magic
Bathed in it
Bubbling beneath my skin
Kissed by it in the moonlight
I was born divine
Royalty
Unique
Set apart
My grandfather told me this
As a little girl
As I sat on his knee
As he would give me peppermints from his pocket
I would look up at him
In awe of his love for me and my worship of him
He smelled of cherry tobacco
I breathed the smell in deeply
It smelled like home
And safety
And love

His hands
Big and strong would take out his pocket watch
And I would rub my tiny hands across it
Mesmerized by the coolness and beauty of it
He was magic
And he told me I was as well
And I believed him
Fully
Completely
Without doubt
He said my magic was a secret
Hidden by the blackness of my skin

In a world that only saw white magic
Obscured by the gentleness of my gender
In a world that only saw greatness in men
But he told me that it was there
Even if others couldn't see it
Even if I couldn't see
It was there
That one day, I would forget
That I was born in magic
Bathed in it
Kissed by it
That I was royalty

Because the world would tell me differently
Every day
That I was less than
Ordinary
Broken
But that one day, I would suddenly remember
These talks
His words
Who I really was
Because I was born in magic
That never dies
Bathed in it
Kissed by it
It bubbles beneath my skin
I was born divine
Royalty
Because I was born in magic

No Reply

No Reply

I love you he says
Then smacks me across my face
I love you he says
Then steals shit out my place
I love you he says
In the midst of another lie
I love you he says
Then wonders why I have no reply

You're the Dopest

You're the dopest
Fyre
And Fire
Flames extend from your very essence
You're the dopest
Honest
Fearless
Fragile
And fierce
Your words breathe life
And set shit on Fire
Your song is like water
Ebbing and flowing
Through the soul of anyone blessed enough to hear it
You don't follow in the footsteps of others
You forge paths that others dream they could follow
Caramel skinned
Blinding smile
Soul dipped in magic

You the fucking dopest
And don't you ever forget it.

Niggas Aint Shit

Niggas ain't shit
I mean
Not *Yo nigga*
Or
All niggas
Just some niggas
And I'm not even talking about race
When I say Nigga
Or culture
Or even gender
I'm talking about niggas
Who ain't shit
Never been shit
Can barely spell shit
Swear they are "The Shit"
But really less than dog shit
I'm talking about Those niggas
That scream call me king
But not worthy to lick the leg of your throne
The ones that say I do
But what they really mean is that I already did

Niggas Aint Shit

Fuck you over
Lie to you
Tear you down
But you just don't know it yet
I'm talking about Those niggas
The ones that still suck at they momma's teet
And what they really want is another momma
To grease they head
And rub they feet
Make them feel like the man
That they'll never be
I'm talking about those niggas
When I say niggas ain't shit
Not yo nigga
Or every nigga

But some niggas
Aint shit

Black Shit

I'm not talking black shit
I'm talking equal rights shit
Justice for all
Not just for yall shit
I'm talking less prison reform
And more police defund
To level the playing field
And don't end in prison in the first shit
I'm not talking black shit
I'm talking about less bodies bloodied in the street
That look like me shit
That if you really believed in God
You wouldn't still be trying to justify owning me shit
I'm not talking about black shit
I'm talking about economic reform
Reparations
Yes, reparations
For years of free labor that keep us poor and made you rich shit
I'm not talking black shit
I'm talking homeless in the streets
while empty buildings are falling apart going to shit, shit

Black Shit

I'm talking lack of access to adequate and affordable healthcare so black and brown are dying way to young unnecessarily shit
I'm talking got the grades but not the funds for education to keep us dumb by design shit
I'm not talking black shit
I'm talking human dignity and quality of life shit

I'm not talking black shit
But if that's all you see

That's all your shit

The Other Side of Here

The Other Side of Here

I don't know what the other side of here looks like
But I do know that it will be better
Full of more hope and promise

I know that I will take the time to enjoy the silence
Amid the chaos that's sure to return
I will live life to its fullest
I will take those trips
I'll accept those invitations to dinner

I will not hide who I am
From myself
Or others

I will hang out more with my children
When they are busy and have no time
I will create time
And space
For us

I am learning Here
In this space of quiet chaos

That life
My life
The life of black folks
Everywhere
Is precious
Finite
Hard
Full of challenge
Painful

But also, beautiful
Exquisite
Creative
Full of promise
On the other side of Here
I will be stronger
My faith will be more intact
I will create the world of kindness that I seek
By understanding when others are rushed
Or in pain
Or sorrow
Or broken
Or alone
That my act of kindness may provide healing
The other side of Here
Is going to be amazing
Because I choose that

The Other Side of Here

Right now
I don't know what tomorrow brings
I leave that to the Lord
That is not my problem
Nor my burden
But my hope
For the other side of Here
Is to be in tune more with His will
His purpose

To live out loud
Not shrinking from who I am
Never taking even the smallest moment for granted
On the other side of here

The World is Burning

The world is burning
I think maybe it's always been
But I never noticed
Not really
Until now
When neighbors
I'd prayed with
Watched their kids
And they'd watched mine
Ate together
Started pulling back
Wearing red caps
Whispered quick hellos and goodbyes
And then stopped speaking at all

The world is burning
I think maybe it's always been
Burning
But I didn't see it
Not really
Until churches started putting up signs that said
We support Blue no matter what
Blue lives Matter
If you don't like America Leave

The world is burning
As it always has
Before I noticed
The Erics
And Sandras
And Trayvons

The world is burning
Always
Burning
Always
Burning
I just didn't notice until now

A Prayer

A Prayer

I look upon the hills
Beyond the shadows
Beyond the darkness of this world
I see my Saviour
I see Him clearly
The Holy One
The Only One
My heart adores
His grace surrounds me
His love abounds me
My heart is full
But my soul begs for more
I fall upon my knees
Shouting Thank You Jesus
The Holy One
The Only One
My heart adores

Tiny World

Tiny World

I look outside my tiny window
To see a tiny world
And look at all the tiny people
Who say such tiny words
Like Hate
And Nigger
And scream with shouts of prejudice
That we don't want you here!
And catchy little phrases
Like, move you fucking queer!
Such tiny words
From tiny people
With tiny little mind
Can damage the heart and souls of man
So please world, let's be kind

Loss

I didn't get to say goodbye
The way I wanted to
I didn't get to say the words of love
I hope you always knew
I didn't get to hold your hand
Or give one last kiss
I didn't get to express to you
How very much you'll be missed
I didn't get to tell you
How much I loved your smile
For one more chance to see your face
I'd gladly walk a mile
I didn't get to share
All my hopes and dreams for you
Oh, how I wish for one more chance
To sit by your side and talk
And have nothing else to do
I wish that you were here
With everything I have
For just one more precious day with you
There's nothing I wouldn't do

Loss

I fall upon my knees
Each and every time I pray
And wish upon wish that day had never come
When you were taken away

And although in time the pain will ease
Because I know you're in a better place
My heart still breaks with every thought of you

Because the kind of love I have for you
Could never be replaced

Lost In The Beat

Lost In The Beat

I bob my head
Lick my lips
Tap my toes
Sway my hips

I let the music fill me
Like a thief, it steals me
I close my eyes
While the rhythm thrills me

I feel the sweat beading
My mind is speeding
Like a lover's kiss
It has my body needing

It takes my hand
Leading me away
All I feel is sound
As the music plays

As it nears the ending
I feel my knees bending
I glance across the room
As my body's descending

Nothing but the vibes
Coming from my shelf
Could make me feel this good
While I'm by myself

The Phone Call

The Phone Call

I received a call today
From a most peculiar man
A collection agent of sorts
Who said my bill was getting out of hand
He began to list my debts
That now seemed were due
He listed lies
Backstabbing
Cheating
Fornication
And a slew of other sins
I begged him to stop
But he just continued
Until my ears ached from the sound within
But then if by magic
His voice did cease
Coming quickly to an abrupt end
He said quite gently
I'm sorry ma'am
I hadn't noticed the note attached to your file's end
Your bill was paid
By Jesus Christ
A most remarkably loving man
He paid blood
By Grace
By Mercy
I shall not be bothering you again.

God Saved Me

God Saved Me

When life seemed too much to bear
God saved me
He brought me through
When rent was due and cupboards were bare
God saved me
He brought me through
When a day without tears seemed awkward and strange
God saved me
He brought me through
When trouble seemed to fall like rain
God saved me
He brought me through
Before I was a though or in my mother's womb
God saved me
He'll save you too

Heartbroken

You broke my heart.
All you who voted for hate.
To make me Less safe than the less safe I already had to endure.
You broke my heart.
All of you Christians who overlooked his flaws of misogyny, hate, xenophobia, sexism, and divisiveness.
Excusing it away.
I don't know the god you serve, but my God and your god must not be the same.
You must feel proud of yourself.
I feel sorry for you. I feel disgusted by you.
But at least I understand clearly where I stand with you.
It's not pretty. And I will not pretend that it is.
You have violated me. Again.
Raped me of my dignity and self-worth.
You have validated to the world that you think of me as less.
That I am unworthy to protect or stand up for.
I will Not go quietly into that good light.
I will fight.
I will be heard.

Heartbroken

I will do what my forefathers did
and what so many failed to do
yesterday.
I Will validate myself.
I Will be heard.
I protect mine.
I will die for that.
I will Not be moved. I will fight.
I will Not go quietly into that good night.
I will kick and scream and fight.
And fight.
And fight.
I will Not live in fear.
And I will Never forget nor forgive this
betrayal of my very existence.

We Used To Be

We used to be tight
Like white on rice
Ticks on skin
Soul within
Tight
We used to be one
Like joined at the hip
You'd swallow when I sipped
So close we read each other's minds not lips
One
We used to be…
But not anymore

Summer

Summer

Jump ropes and jelly shoes
Hide and seek
And peek a boos
Climbing trees and tire swings
Scabbed knees and hula rings
Ice-cold lemonade
On "hot" hot days
Nothing to do but
Play
Play
Play
Mud pies and apple pies
Both ate with zeal
Kickball and volleyball
Playing in the creek
And tumbling down hills
These are the things that made "summer" summer to me

Mother

Mother

How could you not know
How could you not see
That he touched me
In ways that he should never have
That I cried and begged not to go with him
Each time he was at home and left again
That my light dim and shone
Based on his presence
And it felt like
You either didn't see
Or care
Or acknowledge
The fear
The terror
That trebled through my body
That shone within my eyes
That wrapped around me like a second skin
You knew the whispers
Even then
From others
I didn't know then
But you did

Mother

I wouldn't know that until later
That you knew
That friends that I thought no longer wanted to be friends
Were removed from me because of him
That family
Mixed
Mingled
Cousins were brothers
Fathers were uncles
His family history
You knew
And you pretended you didn't
That all the things you heard
Weren't true
That what you saw
So clearly
Couldn't have been
And I hated you for that
He raped me
He didn't touch me
He violently
Viciously

Mother

As if it was his right
Raped me
Took from me
Everything
That was me
But you
You
What you didn't do was so much worse
That somehow even when you knew
And couldn't hide behind saying you didn't
Because everyone knew
Even then
You were not there
As if the pain
And shame
And brokenness
Was too familiar
Too close to what you didn't want to face
Within yourself
So it was easier to leave me broken
Than to have to heal the parts of yourself
You couldn't admit were broken too

Strength through Observation

I found the strength to be myself
Watching you struggle
To be
Someone
You thought others would accept
But you were never created to be

The Gaps You Left Behind

You used to be my everything
My best friend
My all
We exchanged vows
And I exchanged my last name for yours
It wasn't perfect
But it was what it was
Hard
Messy
Full of laughter
And pain
And we shared the joy of seeds
Nurtured in my belly
Being brought forth into life
And you were amazing
With them
Funny
And scared
And vulnerable
But there
Involved
Present
Everyday
You took them to school
And fixed their lunches
You played on the floor in the living room with them

The Gaps You Left Behind

Until way past their bedtimes
We made a lifetime of home movies
And music together
With them
And it was like a constant playdate
For them
But we
No, I
Grew up
And wanted
No, needed
A partner
Not a playmate for the kids
And you couldn't
No wouldn't
Decide to be that
So we broke each other's hearts
And it was painful
But it was over
Had been
For years before it actually was
But I never doubted that you would be there for them
And I was shocked
And hurt
And angry
That you weren't
That you left
And forgot them
Until it was convenient
That you bragged about all you did for them
To others
When you hadn't spoken or seen them in weeks, or months, or years
That you flaunted a life of ease
While your children lived off of meals provided by food banks
And the generosity of others

The Gaps You Left Behind

But not once would I say anything to them
Because they deserved to believe in hope
Of what they once had
So we did it alone
And it was amazing
And they lacked nothing they needed
Even if they didn't always have everything they wanted
And I realized I could fill in the gaps
That you left behind
Or so I thought
Until
Our son needed to learn how to shave
And I cried because I didn't know where to begin
But we sat on the floor of the bathroom
And watched videos of what to do
And we laughed, and I cried
And we practiced with a razor without a blade
And shaving cream was everywhere but where it was supposed to be
And we laughed, and I cried
And hours later
Little nicks covered with bits of toilet paper covered his face
He had done it
We had done it
And he was so proud
And I was so proud of him
And we laughed
And I left him to clean up
And I cried
And my heart broke for him
But I loved him
And loved on him

The Gaps You Left Behind

And covered him in hope and possibility
And I prayed that it was enough
To fill in the gaps that you left behind
Or when our daughter fell in love
For the first time
And when her heart was broken
For the first time
And I held her in my arms
And she cried
And I vowed to hurt the boy who hurt her
But her tears for him turned into tears for you
Why didn't you love her? she sobbed
Why didn't you call or come to see her? she whispered through tears
And I had no answer
But I loved her
And loved on her
And showered her with hope and possibility
And prayed that was enough
To fill in the gaps
That you left behind
And even now
And they are grown
And amazing
And fiercely confident
There are moments
That I see in them
Scars
Openings
Pain
Where they are still trying to fill in
the gaps that you left behind

A View Too Close

It's not all your fault
This ocean of void between us
It's generational
This thing
That causes me to be exhausted by your very presence
This innate desire to love you
Protect you
Pray for you
Want for you what you don't seem to want for yourself
Freedom
Wholeness
Truth
Coupled with this need to protect myself
From you
Your jealousy
Your anger
Your nonsense
The world of make-believe that you build around yourself
And refuse to let falter
For even a second
Truth is not a concept that you find easy
Not really
Although you demand it
From others
But not yourself

Loving you is messy
And hard
And nothing I can do anymore
Not up close and personal
It takes too much from me
And that breaks my heart
But it's not all your fault
Not completely
I saw it happening
For years
We all did
Those that say they love you
And said nothing
And did nothing
Because we loved you
We told ourselves
But really, we were just cowards
Afraid to get involved
Afraid of what it would cost
In time
In money
In our own sense of peace
And sanity
I was
We all were
Too afraid of stepping in
And forcing conversations that we knew would be
Exhaustive
Draining
So we hoped
And pretended with you
Because we wanted to believe it was true
This time
That you were getting better
This time
Having conversations on the side

Of the illness that was overtaking you
Had overtaken you
Destroying you
While you pretended it didn't exist
And it was easier for us to close our eyes
And pretend with you
Until we couldn't anymore
You deserved more
From me
From all of us
You deserved more from me
And I'm sorry that I wasn't strong enough to give you that
And I deserved more of myself
And I regret that I didn't know that then
The boundaries that blurred
Over and over again

The broken promises
The lack of trust
All covered with a smile and a laugh
That hid tears
And hurt
And pain
Because it wasn't you
It was this illness
That we saw glimpses of
In generations past
That no one wanted to talk about
That remained an open secret
Of shame
Of fear
That we refused to acknowledge
Because we knew it could easily be any of us
So we ignored it
Because it was easier
Until it wasn't

I Can't With You

I can't with you
Because I would want more
Than I have a right to expect
And would settle for
Less
Than I deserve
And I can't do that again

Perspective

Perspective

When I look at a dandelion
I can choose to see
The weed that it is
Or the beautiful flowing seeds
Dozens of wishes
Waiting to be fulfilled

Longing

Longing

*I don't want to be
Just a passing*
Random
Fleeting
Afterthought
For you
*I want to be
Your early morning*
Late at night
Bring a smile to your face
And a tingle down your spine
Every thought

Thoughts of You

I thought of you today
And it made me smile
And that smile
Sent a tingle
Unexpected
Yet welcomed
Down my spine
And that tingle
Tickled my toes
And that tickle
Made me smile
And think of you.

Finding Out

It was an open secret
That I didn't quite belong
That there was a part of me that I would never really know
The first time it was spoken aloud
To me
Was at my grandfather's funeral
A close distant relative
Approached me
And smiled
And said, "Look at you"
"Looking just like..."
I'm not sure that it registered with me
Not really
Or I was so accustomed to pretending
That this thing
Wasn't a thing
That I don't even think I responded
But I remember it clearly
And it stuck with me
And nudged me
And pushed me
To finally ask
This thing that I shouldn't have ever had to ask
Who was my father?

Finding Out...

This thing that I've always known was unknown
This thing that my mother felt was her business
And none of my mine
But I had a right to know
Didn't I?
I felt I didn't
Not really
It was such a heavy secret
That everyone carried
It hovered over the room when I entered
It cloaked me with its lack of existence
It suffocated me with the weight of a shame that wasn't mine
It just was
It would still be years later
After my grandfather's funeral
before I would know
Something
But still
Really nothing
I would be a mother myself
Fiercely protective of my own children
Nurturing them through a broken relationship with their own father
But still, this part of me
This known unknow
Open secret
Part of who I was
Would always be lost
Childlike

Finding Out...

Part of me wishing I had never known
Would never know
My mother told me through a phone call
That she wasn't sure who my father was
But that she was almost certain that I was a product of
rape
Her stepbrother
My uncle
She said she was mostly certain
That she never wanted to speak it aloud
Didn't want to acknowledge it
That she had felt shame
And never wanted to tell me
But had to
Finally
After years of whispers
And pain
Through a phone call
Her voice
Seemed far
And near
Loud
And soft
Her words
Seemed to move too fast
And drawn out
All at the same time
I was angry
And hurt
And numb

Finding Out...

I remember at some point I could no longer hear her
Her words
Foreign and familiar
Felt like knives in my ears
I drove around for hours
And hours
And cried
And screamed
And then nothing
I
Felt
Nothing
This secret
This burden
This shame
Did not lift
Finding out
Did not free me
As I had hoped
As I had prayed for
Finding out
Simply
Quietly
Wrapped me in lost
Hung heavy in the air
Cloaked me in shame
And buried me deeper in pain

Moonlight Dance

Moonlight Dance

I want to dance in the moonlight
I want to bask in the sun
I want to splash around and play in the rivers of old
I want to intertwine my fingers in the cool clay of which Adam was formed
I want to smile and laugh while sitting at the feet of my ancestors
Listening to them tell me of love and pain and triumph and struggle
I want to sleep in the fields with the night sky above
Clothed in the grace and protection of God
I want to take a break from this world
Full of hate
Full of hurt
Full of pain
Full of things that threaten to drown out beauty
Full of things that threaten to drown out peace
Full of things that seem to drown out love
For ourselves
For one another
Just for today
I want to hear no more of war
Of hate
Of bigotry
Of why you justify it with religion
Or patriotism
Or fear
Or anything
Just for today, I want to live inside the poems of my ancestors
That spoke of beauty and peace and love
That spoke of freedom and equality
That spoke of earth and sky
Like they were sacred things to be treasured and protected
Just for today
I want to dance in the moonlight and bask in the sun and splash around and play in the rivers of old.

Unbreaking Brokenness

Finding me
No, facing those parts of me
Pieces
Hidden
Buried
Broken
Shattered
Pieces
Of what makes me whole
The pain
And joy
The tears
And laughter
Not diminishing one over the other
Slowly
Carefully
Like pieces of a puzzle
Fitting together
Shaping itself
Into completeness

MOTHER OF THE GROOM

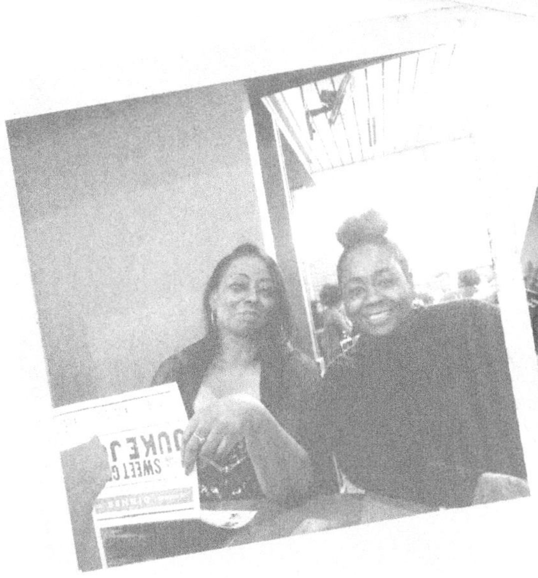

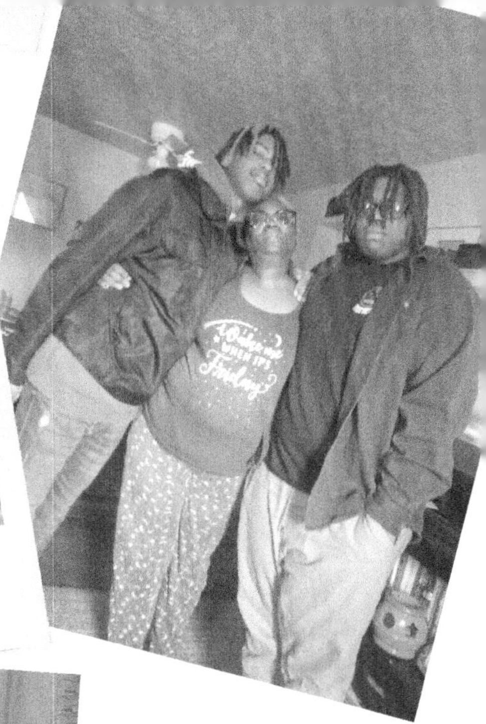

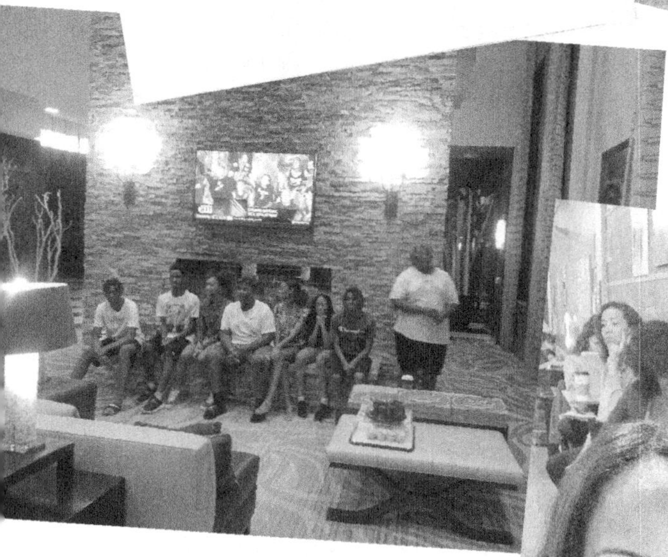

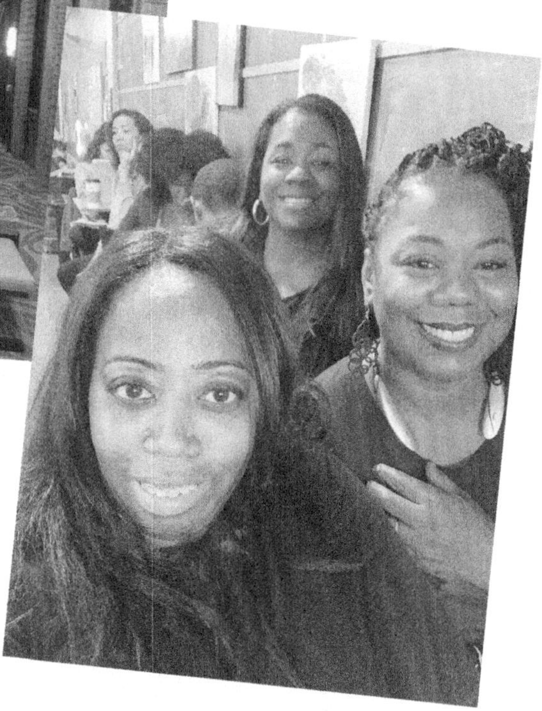

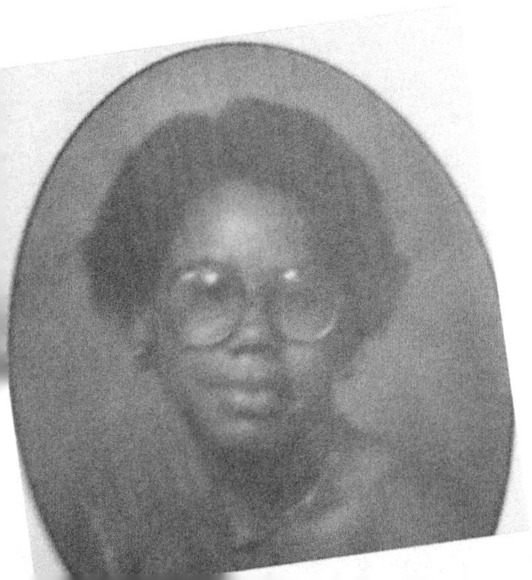

Acknowledgements

    I want to thank God first for continuing to sew possibility, purpose, and passion within me even when I couldn't recognize it was there.

To Pastor Steve - who showed me by example how to truly come to Christ just as I was and feel not only accepted but acceptable just as I am.

Thank you, Kiwi, Kenny, Kevon, Kaiden, and Kameron, for being the best and most supportive kids anyone could ever hope for. You all make me better, stronger, more capable of love each and every day. I don't deserve the gift of each of you, but I'm so very grateful for it.

To my sisters - what a journey our lives have been. Thank you for your love. It's carried me farther than you'll ever know.

To my sister/cousin Chrissy - anyone lucky enough to know you and your fiercely protective and loyal love is blessed beyond measure. I love you girl!

To my mom - who would have ever thought we'd be here. Together. I thank God for the restoration. And I thank God for you.

To Candace - sisters from the moment we met. I love you more than words can express, and I am grateful for your friendship and love through the years.

To Bill - The seed you sowed of possibility in me so many years ago has stayed with me and grown in ways I could have never imagined. You were the first to say that it was okay to expect more, dream too big. Thank you for encouraging me to see more than just the world around me.

To Bubbalicious - you know who you are and you know what it is! And you know that I love you more than the sun and the moon and everything in between. Thank you for reminding me that I'm His favorite even when I forget.

To my family and friends and those that have crossed my path in those God moments that pushed me and believed in me and kept encouraging me to Just Do It Already!

Thank you!

I finally did!

Keneatha Renae

About the Author

Keneatha lives in Georgia. Passionate about racial and social justice and giving voice to those who don't feel like they have one because of having lost her own for far too long. Not religious but deeply spiritual. A Christ-follower choosing to walk in love in a world filled with hate. A single mom of one amazing black queen and four dope black kings. They are her life, and everything she does is in service to the gift of them.

BLACK & BARE PRESS

Made in the USA
Columbia, SC
24 October 2024